Look and Find
BATMAN™

Written by Joe Edkin

Illustrated by Jaime Diaz Studios

Cover penciled by Graham Nolan
Cover inked by Scott Hanna

Scenes 1 and 2 colored by Adrienne Roy

Published by
Louis Weber, C.E.O.
Publications International, Ltd.
7373 North Cicero Avenue
Lincolnwood, Illinois 60646

Manufactured in U.S.A.

8 7 6 5 4 3 2 1

ISBN 0-7853-1353-2

PUBLICATIONS INTERNATIONAL, LTD.

ROBIN'S AUDIO JOURNAL. NEW YEAR'S EVE. 10:00 P.M.
THE NEWS JUST CAME FROM POLICE COMMISSIONER GORDON. IT SEEMS THE PENGUIN HAS OFFERED US A CHALLENGE. WE'VE GOT JUST TWO HOURS TO FIND AND CAPTURE SOME OF GOTHAM CITY'S MOST DANGEROUS CRIMINALS, INCLUDING TWO-FACE. HE'S MADE HIS MOVE BY ATTACKING THE GOTHAM CITY CAR SHOW AT THE CIVIC CENTER.

Before they leave the Batcave, Batman and Robin must collect the equipment they may need tonight. Help them prepare for the Penguin's challenge by finding the following:

Spikes

Blankets

Batarang

Handcuffs

Gas mask

Smoke pellets

Antidote

Net

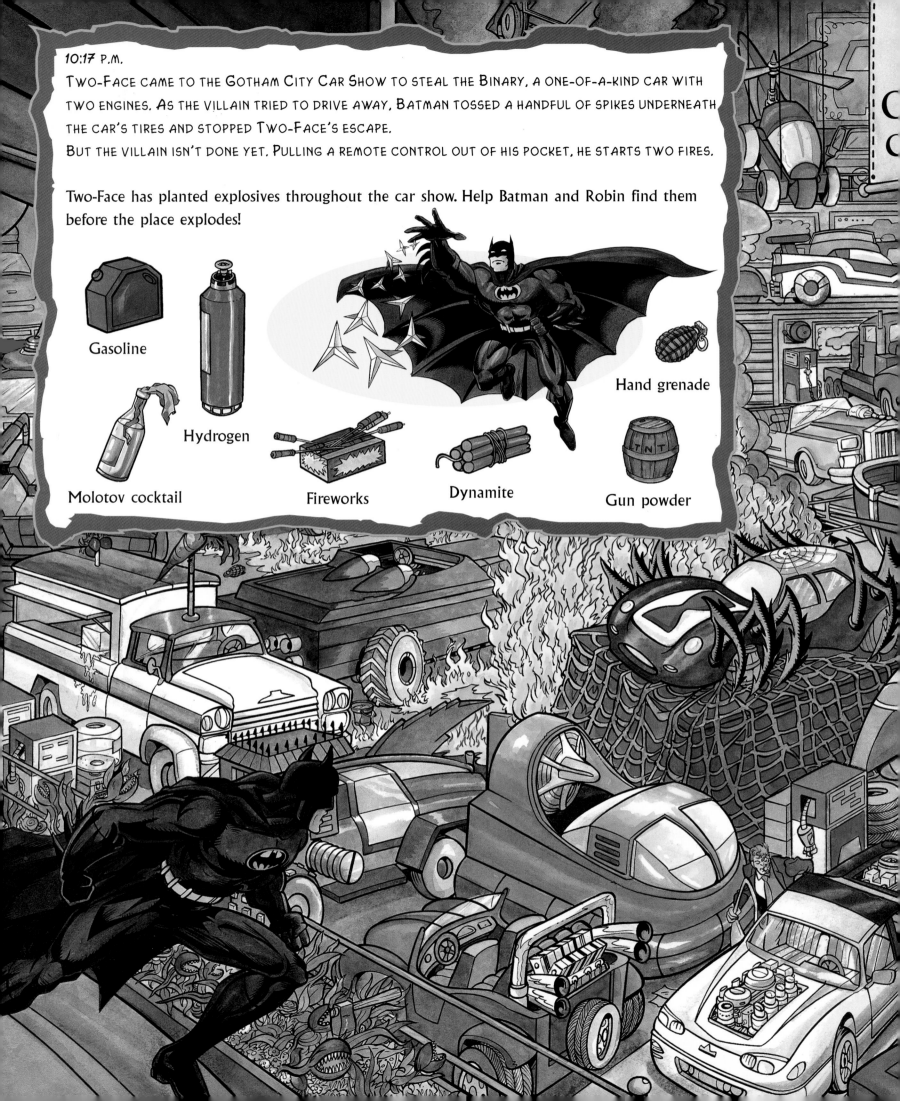

10:17 P.M.

TWO-FACE CAME TO THE GOTHAM CITY CAR SHOW TO STEAL THE BINARY, A ONE-OF-A-KIND CAR WITH TWO ENGINES. AS THE VILLAIN TRIED TO DRIVE AWAY, BATMAN TOSSED A HANDFUL OF SPIKES UNDERNEATH THE CAR'S TIRES AND STOPPED TWO-FACE'S ESCAPE.

BUT THE VILLAIN ISN'T DONE YET. PULLING A REMOTE CONTROL OUT OF HIS POCKET, HE STARTS TWO FIRES.

Two-Face has planted explosives throughout the car show. Help Batman and Robin find them before the place explodes!

Gasoline

Hydrogen

Molotov cocktail

Fireworks

Dynamite

Hand grenade

Gun powder

10:34 P.M.

TWO-FACE IS WITH THE POLICE. OUR NEXT STOP IS RIVERFRONT PARK, WHERE SOME OF GOTHAM CITY'S CITIZENS ARE ENJOYING A NEW YEAR'S EVE PARTY. MR. FREEZE IS PLANNING TO ROB THE PARTYGOERS. HE HAS HIDDEN SEVEN FREEZING DEVICES THROUGHOUT THE PARK AND HAS USED THE MACHINES TO CAPTURE SEVERAL PEOPLE IN ICE.

Help Batman and Robin find the freezing devices so they can rescue Mr. Freeze's victims and capture the villain.

10:46 P.M.

AFTER HANDING OVER MR. FREEZE TO THE POLICE, BATMAN AND I FOLLOWED SEVERAL SUSPICIOUS CLUES TO SCHIFF'S TOY SHOP, WHERE WE CAUGHT THE RIDDLER IN THE MIDDLE OF A ROBBERY. AS WE CUFFED THE CROOK, THE RIDDLER JUST LAUGHED AND HANDED US A NOTE:

Piano

Beehive

Jelly beans

Zebra

Bloodhound

Submarine sandwich

Batman:

If you can't solve the following riddles, it could have explosive results. Hope you don't blow it! —R.

What kind of dog did Dracula keep as a pet?

The alphabet goes from A to Z. What goes from Z to A?

How does a queen bee wear her hair?

What kind of beans aren't good for you?

What has 88 keys but can't unlock any doors?

What kind of submarine can you eat?

The Riddler has rigged the store with hidden bombs! Batman and Robin have solved the riddles and figured out which objects are booby traps. Can you find them all?

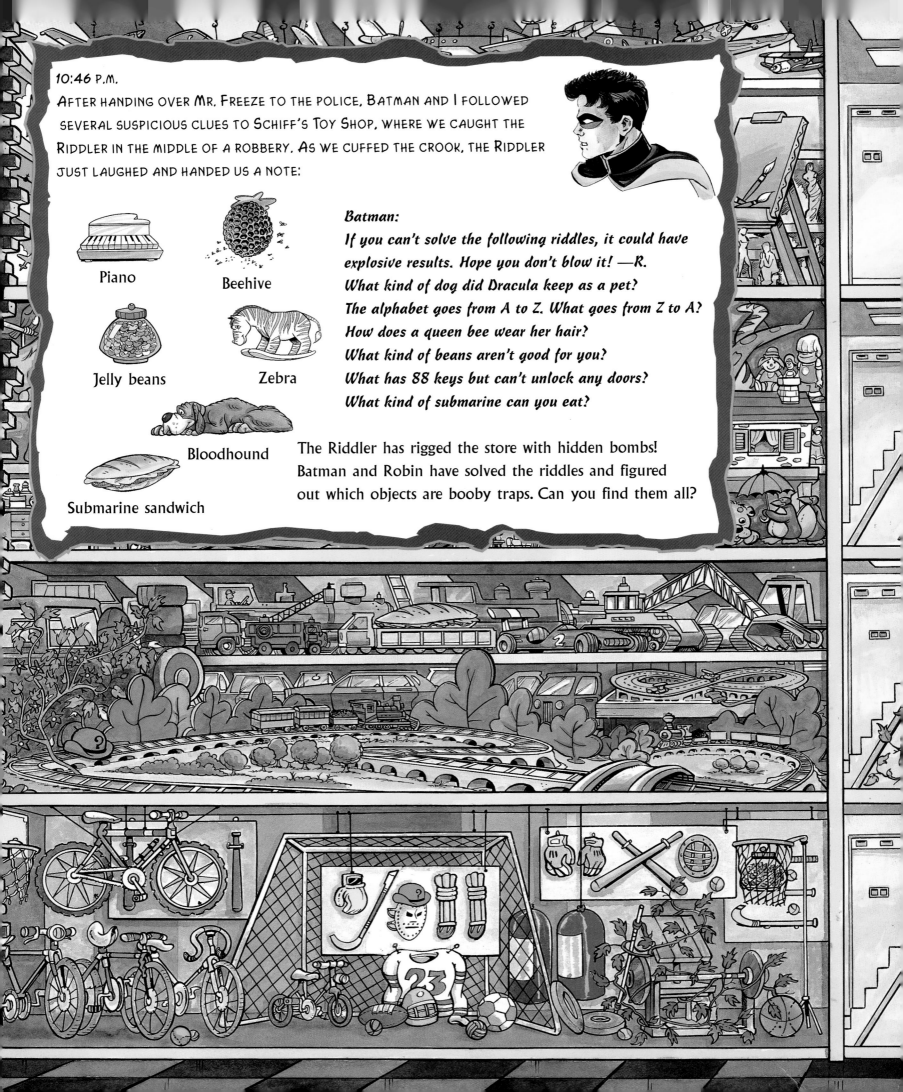

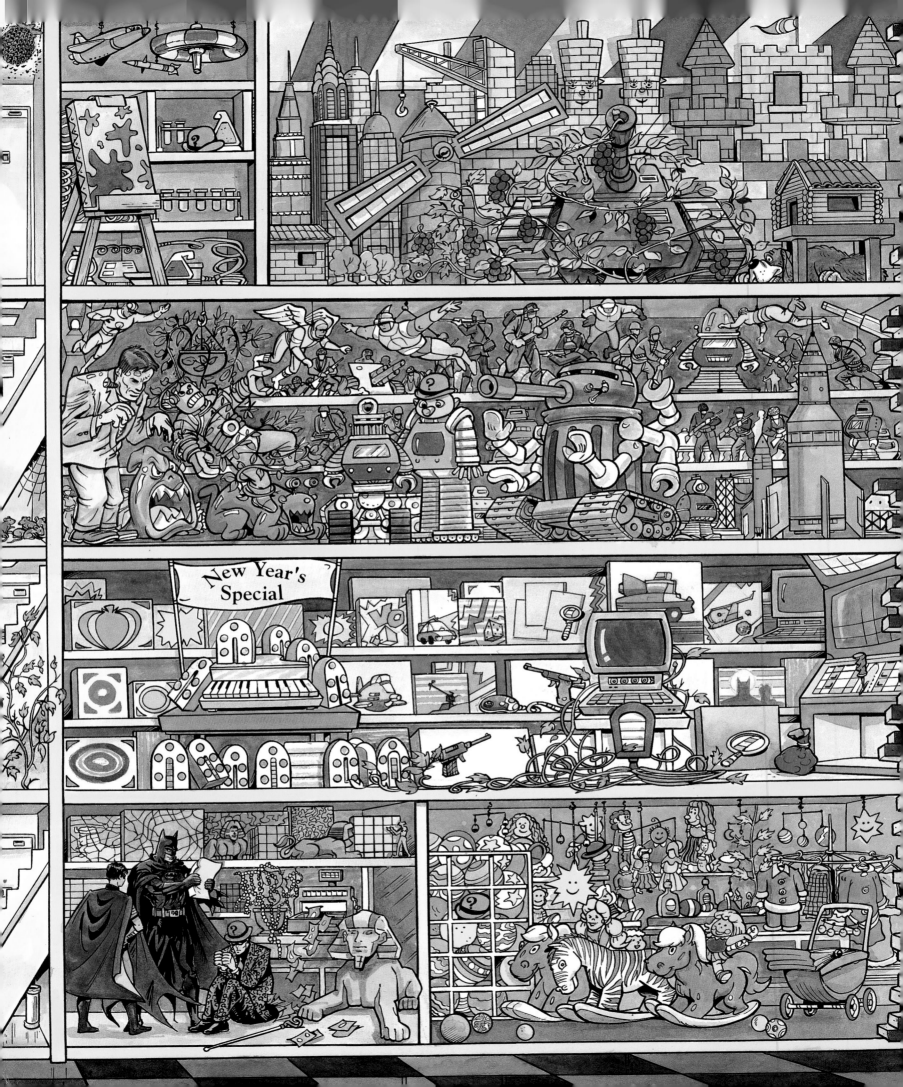

11:00 P.M.

THE RIDDLER'S BOMBS ARE DISARMED AND THE VILLAIN IS ON HIS WAY BACK TO HIS CELL. BUT THIS NIGHT ISN'T OVER YET! POISON IVY HAS BROKEN INTO THE GOTHAM BOTANICAL GARDENS TO STEAL THE RARE HYBRID BLUE SAPPHIRE ROSE. SHE'S TIED UP EIGHT GUARDS AND LEFT THEM WITHIN REACH OF SEVERAL DEADLY GIANT VENUS'S-FLYTRAPS!

Help Batman and Robin find the eight security guards and the Blue Sapphire Rose so they can stop Poison Ivy.

Charlie

Michael

Jennifer

Ann

Scott

Michelle

Greg

Sarah

Blue Sapphire Rose

11:13 P.M.

POISON IVY IS SAFELY IN POLICE CUSTODY, BUT THE SCARECROW HAS MADE HIS WAY INTO ONE OF THE SCIENCE LABS AT GOTHAM STATE UNIVERSITY TO STEAL A FRESH SUPPLY OF THE CHEMICALS THAT HE USES TO MAKE HIS FEAR GAS.

AS WE ENTER THE ROOM, THE SCARECROW TRIGGERS SEVERAL SKULL-SHAPED DEVICES TO SPRAY THE FEAR GAS, WHICH CREATES THE ILLUSION THAT WE ARE SURROUNDED BY AN ARMY OF OUR ENEMIES!

Help Batman and Robin find the skulls spraying the fear gas, so they can break the illusion and capture the real villain here.

11:29 P.M.

WITH THE SCARECROW BEHIND BARS, A SERIES OF CLUES HAS LED US TO OUR NEXT DESTINATION—
KING SOLOMON'S DIAMOND EXCHANGE. CATWOMAN, THE WORLD'S GREATEST CAT BURGLAR, HAS HER
SIGHTS SET ON STEALING THE ENORMOUS HYPE DIAMOND ON DISPLAY HERE. BUT SHE IS NOT ALONE; SHE
HAS SEVERAL OF HER CATS, AND ONE VERY HUNGRY LION, WITH HER! WHILE WE DEAL WITH THE LION, THE
CATS ARE MAKING OFF WITH VALUABLE JEWELS.

Help Batman and Robin recover the Hype Diamond and round up Catwoman's feline friends.

Fluffy

Butch

Hype Diamond

Spot

Whiskers

Mittens

Maisie

11:41 P.M.

CATWOMAN IS WITH THE POLICE, AND THE LION IS BACK IN HIS CAGE AT THE CIRCUS. BATMAN AND I ARE HERE, TOO—IN HOT PURSUIT OF THE JOKER! THE CLOWN PRINCE OF CRIME IS PLANNING TO WREAK HAVOC AT THE CIRCUS'S NEW YEAR'S EVE PERFORMANCE. HE HAS HIDDEN FIVE BOMBS AND PLANTED SIX OF HIS THUGS IN THE CROWD.

Help Batman and Robin nab the Joker by locating the bombs and finding the thugs disguised as clowns.

Hector

Bomb

Nikki

Verna

Wilbur

Fingers

Rocko

11:59 P.M.

WE FINALLY CAUGHT UP WITH THE MASTERMIND BEHIND TONIGHT'S MAYHEM—THE PENGUIN—AT THE GOTHAM MUSEUM OF CINEMATIC ARTS. THE VILLAIN BOASTED THAT HE HELPED THE OTHERS ESCAPE FROM THEIR CELLS, AND THEN LEFT A SERIES OF CLUES AT THE SITE OF EACH CRIME TO LEAD US FROM ONE CROOK TO THE NEXT. THE PENGUIN GAMBLED THAT WE WOULD BE EXHAUSTED BY THE TIME WE REACHED HIM, AND THAT HE WOULD WIN HIS GAME OF WITS.

The Penguin has rigged a number of booby traps in the museum. Batman and Robin have to find and disarm the traps, so they can capture the Penguin and put an end to this New Year's night of crime.

Trip wire

Trap door

Bomb

Laser gun

Guillotine

Rocket launcher

Screening Room

ROBIN GAVE HIS AUDIO JOURNAL TO COMMISSIONER GORDON TO HELP HIM PREPARE HIS POLICE REPORT ON THE CRIME WAVE. THE COMMISSIONER NEEDED TO KNOW HOW THE HEROES WERE ABLE TO CAPTURE ALL THE VILLAINS SO QUICKLY. THE JOURNAL EXPLAINED THAT THE PENGUIN HAD LEFT BEHIND A SERIES OF CLUES. CAN YOU GO BACK AND FIND ALL THE CLUES BATMAN AND ROBIN USED TO CAPTURE THE VILLAINS?

THE PENGUIN THINKS HE'S PLAYING A GAME WITH BATMAN AND ROBIN. SEE IF YOU CAN FIND THE FOLLOWING ITEMS IN THE BATCAVE THAT ARE ALSO USED IN OTHER GAMES:

- ☐ PLAYING DICE
- ☐ A JOKER CARD
- ☐ CHESS PIECES
- ☐ EIGHT BALL
- ☐ BASEBALL BAT
- ☐ BOWLING PIN
- ☐ CROSSWORD PUZZLE

AT THE CAR SHOW, THE PENGUIN LEFT BEHIND THE FOLLOWING CLUES TO LEAD BATMAN AND ROBIN TO MR. FREEZE AT RIVERFRONT PARK. CAN YOU FIND THEM ALL?

- ☐ BLOCK OF ICE
- ☐ FROZEN FISH
- ☐ SAILING BOAT
- ☐ TUG BOAT
- ☐ ANCHOR
- ☐ DIAMONDS

AT RIVERFRONT PARK, THE PENGUIN LEFT BEHIND THESE CLUES TO LEAD BATMAN AND ROBIN TO THE RIDDLER AT SCHIFF'S TOY SHOP. THE CLUES ALL HAVE QUESTION MARKS ON THEM. CAN YOU FIND THEM ALL?

- ☐ JIGSAW PUZZLE
- ☐ TEDDY BEAR
- ☐ PUZZLE CUBE
- ☐ BICYCLE
- ☐ TOY DUMP TRUCK
- ☐ SPHINX

AT THE TOY SHOP, THE PENGUIN LEFT BEHIND THESE LEAFY CLUES TO LEAD BATMAN AND ROBIN TO POISON IVY. CAN YOU FIND THEM ALL?

- ☐ A GREEN VINE
- ☐ A VINE WITH RED FLOWERS
- ☐ AN ORANGE VINE
- ☐ A VINE WITH PURPLE BERRIES
- ☐ A BLUE VINE
- ☐ A MULTICOLORED VINE